Dream The Impossible Dream
Yvonne Pointer
1-18-99

Behind the Death of a Child

Yvonne Pointer

Illustrations by Khaz Ra'el
(Donald Cassidy)

KENDALL/HUNT PUBLISHING COMPANY
4050 Westmark Drive   Dubuque, Iowa   52002

In Loving Memory
Gloria Pointer
1970–1984

This book is dedicated in the precious memories of my beloved daughter, Gloria Pointer, who was so brutally slain on December 6, 1984. Dedicated to those of you who understand firsthand, through possible similar experiences what the lines in this book represent. I am indeed very thankful for my family, my pastor, Elder James Boyd, and his wife, Mattie, and all my friends who were here for me, and most of all I am thankful for my Heavenly Father who held my hand through one of the most tragic ordeals in my life, and did not leave me alone.

Contents

Part I—The Crime   1

Part II—The Anguish   27

Part III—The Mother—A Very Special Lady   49

Preface

Behind the Death of a Child is a poetic expression of literature depicting the suffering and agony suffered by a mother who lost her oldest daughter to a brutal act of violence. It reveals how the mother, Yvonne Pointer, reacted and coped with the death of her daughter, and the stages she endured while coping and learning from her grief.

The death of Yvonne's daughter was a senseless act. Her loss and the barbaric separation from her daughter were just as painful and laborious as was the "birth of her child." Unlike the birth process though, death by brutality always leaves lingering questions of "How could this have happened to such an innocent child?", "Who could have done such an act," and "What could they have done to prevent it?" Facing the mother are endless hours of grief and anger while she waits for justice. She knows no peace. Peace is a luxury which only comes with time.

Behind the Death of a Child is also a symbolic, pictorial, and poetic representation for every mother that loses a child to the hands of death. Every hour, every minute of every day, death occurs and a mother must find the strength to overcome her loss. The pain is still the same regardless of the race, creed, color, or age. The agony and the anguish each mother experiences, feels the same. Death, regardless of the circumstances, makes a mother wonder why it did not happen to her instead.

This book will make you cry and feel remorse not only for the child but for the mother that has to endure the grief of losing her child. It is also a book that will guide you to a stage of strength and profound faith in the Will of the Most High God. "All things happen for a reason," even the reason *Behind the Death of a Child.*

Sincerely,
Barbara Johnson

Foreword

I met Yvonne Pointer in late 1984 when I was a State Senator. At the time, I had just finished a year-long effort on behalf of Ohio's Missing Children's Act, a bill I had authored and which the General Assembly approved in December, 1984.

During the year of debate surrounding the bill, I had heard and read many stories of the grief caused when a child is missing. All of them affected me very deeply. But when I heard the story of Yvonne and Gloria, my heart went out to them in a very special way.

During the rest of the time I spent in the General Assembly, I kept in touch with Yvonne and learned from her how she was dealing with the tragedy that is every parent's worst nightmare. I have been proud over the past decade to be Yvonne's friend, employer and student. I say student because there have been many times that Yvonne has taught me something new about myself, my community and about the responsibility those of us in public office have.

After a long and close race for Attorney General in 1990—the closest statewide race in Ohio history, in fact—I asked Yvonne to give a few remarks at my inauguration. Her words of support and encouragement have stayed with me. Yvonne has been a loyal and hard-working member of my staff ever since.

Compiling these poems and stories about a mother's coping with the senseless loss of a child helped Yvonne, and they can be a source of comfort to the other parents who face the tragedy of losing a child. They also provide a window into her soul so you can see the inner beauty and strength that I have come to see in Yvonne.

Yvonne is a very special person to me. She's special because of the harmony she creates between her job and her life experiences. She has an enviable ability to help her connect with people from all walks of life, whether they are a victim of a crime, a young child learning about drug education, or a public official whose feet need to be kept to the fire. She's an extraordinary asset to our office and, I believe, to the state of Ohio.

I hope you enjoy reading these works.

Sincerely,
Former Attorney General,
State of Ohio
Lee Fisher

Introduction

What a woman of stature and courage, this is what I thought when my eyes first fell upon Yvonne Pointer. It was a sunny, but cold and remorseful day and I was attending the funeral of Gloria Pointer, Yvonne's 14-year-old daughter. I am the detective assigned to assist in the homicidal investigation of this child. This church was filled with friends and relatives of the deceased and I watched Gloria's classmates filled with anguish and sorrow over her hideous death. As I scoured through the faces of those attending, I was drawn to Yvonne's large intense brown eyes searching the different faces of the mourners as they walked past the casket. She sat erect and smiled occasionally, but searched continually for a possible suspect that had the gall to attend her daughter's funeral.

Gloria's life was snatched away when she was brutally raped and murdered on December 6, 1984. It was a cold and blustery morning. Gloria left home 15 minutes early without her mother's permission. She was to receive an award for good attendance and punctuality that day at school. Gloria had made arrangements to meet at her friend's house and the two would walk to school together.

The school notified Yvonne of Gloria's absence at 8:00 a.m. Two hours later Gloria's body was found in the rear of an apartment building next to the school. Gloria never made it to her girlfriend's house. This murder is still unsolved.

Through the years I have shared and learned so much from this brave woman. Yvonne has progressed not regressed. Behind the death of her child, she has gone out into the world helping others. Upon learning the deaths of other children, she has gone to the aid of other parents, sharing her experiences in how she coped with the tragic loss of a loved one. She has formed and joined other support groups. Yvonne has counseled hundreds of children and set up preventive programs to insure the safety of our children in the streets. Yvonne has turned her life over to Jesus Christ. She hasn't become complacent to wait on a miracle. She continues to fast, and through faith and prayer she is working toward her miracle. We haven't given up hope to find Gloria's murderer. I keep a picture of Gloria on my desk to constantly remind me that her killer is loose on the street. It is an honor to know Yvonne Pointer. My admiration is due to her unyielding faith that God will answer our prayers. The following pages will reveal Yvonne's inner most emotions and feelings that may have been shared by many . . . *Behind the Death of a Child.*

Janice Abernathy

Mommy, Speak For Me...

Mommy speak for me,
Tell the world of the pain
That I felt with the blow to my head
As he left my body in the rain

Mommy speak for me,
Even though my body is not there
Please find someone who will listen
There must be someone, somewhere

Mommy speak for me,
Not just for me, myself and I
For there are so many children like myself
Who want to know the reason why

Mommy speak for me,
For was I bad, did I deserve to die that way?
Maybe you can get someone to tell you
Why children are abused in the world today

Mommy, and if they won't listen
Don't hang your head in shame
Just always know that I love you
And you did try, just the same.

Part I

The Crime

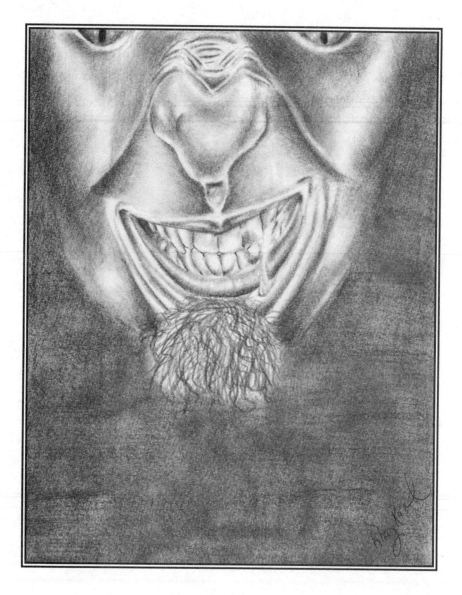

Killer Loose in the City

Did you know that he is still at large
The one who thrives off the blood of young innocent girls
You may know him, you may have seen him
Sneaking down the long alley between hell and here

Who's looking for him, I am, are you?
Who wants to live in the city where a killer is loose?
Together we can find him, together we can capture him

He is cold, he has no heart, it turned to ice a long
    time ago
Conscience, what is that, it was seared from his birth
He is what you call scum, slime, and filth
Oh, I know that he is someone's son
Nevertheless, he is still a *Killer Loose in the City*

He sucks blood, did you know that?
Did you know that he has formed an appetite for the
    blood of your daughter.
The color red is his favorite color,
Next to green which is the color of the money
That buys the dope for his habit.

I talked to the dope man
I told him about the *Killer Loose in the City*
I called him the killer, when I caught up with him
Between here and California
Sipping tall drinks, fondling pretty women, and driving
   Cadillacs
Told that dope man to leave our children alone

I want to tell the killer to leave our children alone
Only I can't find him, no one knows where I can find him
Or should I say no one will tell me where to find him
They know, someone knows, but won't tell
You know why? Because they are the killers too
For they hide the *Killer Loose in the City!*

Is There Any News Yet

Be patient, be patient,
I know, but is there any news yet
Too many days have gone by
The trail will have ice over it
Maybe it is just me, maybe my days seem like years
Maybe it just seems as if it is taking forever

It is forever, look at how long it has been
My hands sweat, my heart races, everytime the phone
    rings
Hello, Mr. Detective, Hello, Ms. Detective, *Is There Any*
    News Yet
Are you calling to tell me, that you have him
That he's off the streets so he can't kill again

Mamma wants to know, do you have him
Sisters and brothers want to know do you have him
I want to know are there any leads, what about
    confessions
Are you afraid that I will be afraid
Is that why I don't hear from you
I won't, I've met fear, I'm not afraid of him
He's only a figment of my imagination

So go ahead and tell me
Is There Any News Yet?

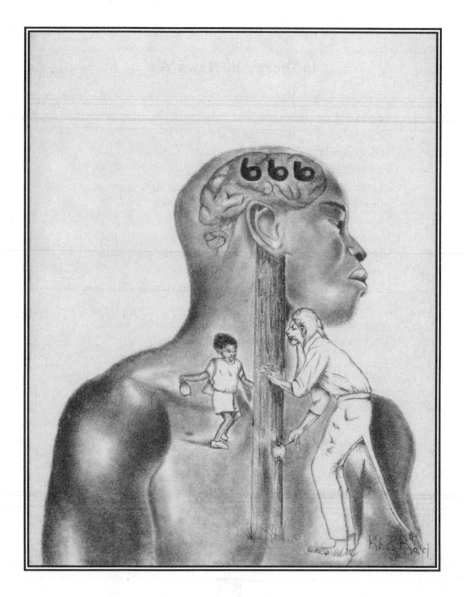

Beware Little Girls

What should you do, should you stay locked in the house
Should you hide under the bed, hide behind the skirt tails
   of mamma
Maybe even put your head beneath the sand until he's off
   the streets

Oh!, how I wish I could walk with you—all of you
I wish I could protect you from him—all of you
I wish I could make this world a safer place for you—
All of you

But I can't, you see I am not God and He did not leave
   me in charge
I need Him to walk with me—just as you do
I need Him to protect me—just as you do
I need Him to make it better for me—just as you do

Beware little girls that the wicked one
Who lurks the streets does not get you
He's not only out there, he's inside too
He's waiting on you to forget your safety teachings
He's waiting on you to be silly and get in his car
To eat his candy, to accept his money

Beware, don't you do it
Come back, come back to where I am
Maybe God will let me protect you until He comes to
    take us away
Maybe I can be your eyes to see that wicked one from afar
    off
I didn't recognize him with Gloria
But I know him now, his type, that is
He lurks, he hides, he peeps, he slithers just like a snake
Beware Little Girls
And remember that God will watch out for you
And so will I!

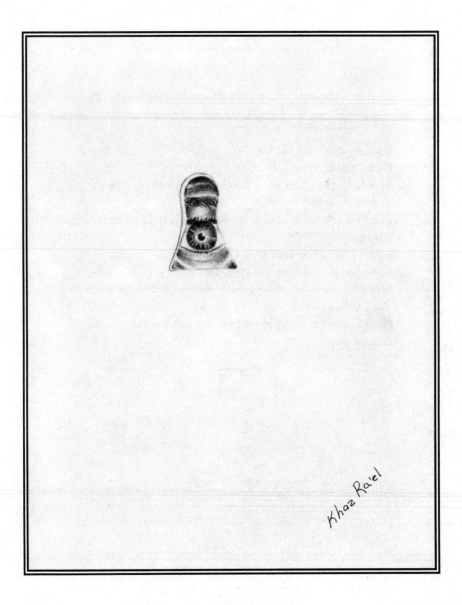

Who Did It?

Who did it?
Who did it, did you?
Did you swing the final blow that took the last breath
  away
Was it you that held the metal pipe between your fingers
Are you the one who heard the final screams,
The last plea

How do you sleep now, how do you feel now
I wonder, I ponder over who did it
Was mamma help me, the words that slip from the edge
  of her lips as she went
Did she see your face,
Does she know your name,
Did you do it

Maybe you didn't do it
Maybe you heard her screams as you rolled over for your
  second sleep
Maybe you saw him as he laid the pipe to her skull
Maybe it was you who said I don't want to get involved
Maybe it was you who looked through your peephole to
  see his size
To see his shape, to see his face
As he slithered back into his hiding hole

Maybe it was you who did it,
Who saw but say nothing
Yes it was you,
You who continue to do it by not saying anything
I know who did it,
You did because you don't get involved
Because you are afraid that if you say, then you will get it
I've met fear, I know that he keeps you bound if you let
   him

Don't be afraid, say it if you know it,
Shout it, tell it
And let's get who did it
So that we all can sleep
So that we all can rest
So that we all can put a period at the end.

Call Them in the Middle of the Night

We can be reached in the middle of the night
when no one else will be bothered
You are not alone, so call them in the middle of the night
when the awful memories of the crime committed
against you resound in your sleep
When you scream into the pillow, leave me alone.
Please don't kill me.

Why do you want to rape me,
My dress isn't too short
My jeans aren't tight, my blouse isn't cut low
Why do you want to wrap your hands around my throat
I am not bothering anyone, I am on my way to work
to make a living for my five small children
My husband left, and I'm all alone, why bother me

Please don't do this, please don't do this!
You say don't scream, don't run, don't resist,
You will rape me and go down the
Street and rape again
You won't kill me, you say
You just want to show me and all of them
Who is the boss

How horrible, How awful it was that night
Who can I call when the memories of the crime
Committed against me resound in my sleep
Who can I call when I am angry, when I am mad
When I feel dirty, when I feel low and sad

I've heard of a place that I can call and they will under-
  stand
That I am the victim, I am the victim, not him
They will understand that it was me who suffered a
Great injustice, not him
Oh, he doesn't have to suffer like me, he has so much
  protection
Who will plead my cause

I'll call . . . I'll tell . . . it's me whose having trouble
  sleeping
In the middle of the night when the memories of the
Crime committed against me resound in my sleep
What is that number of
THE RAPE CRISIS CENTER
They said that I can *Call Them in the Middle of the Night!*
Consult your local listing

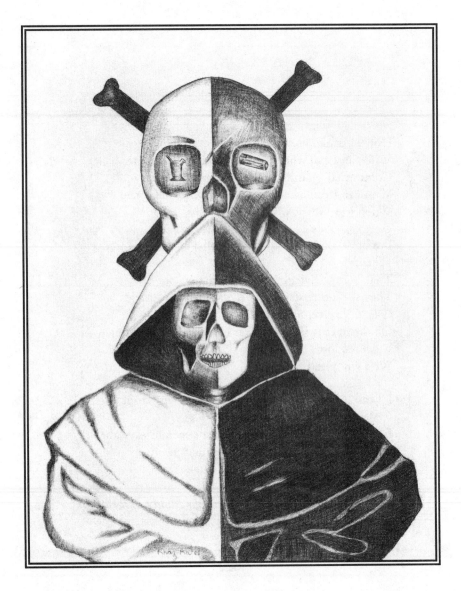

Hey Mr. Dope Man

Hey, Mr. Dope Man, can I rap with you for a minute
I want to tell you a story about a little girl that you killed
Oh!, you say that you ain't killed no little girl
Oh!, you say that on the day she was killed you were kick-
    ing up your heels
Kicking your heels up under the sunny skies of California
Spending big money, driving big Cadillacs and
Fondling pretty women

Having big fun off the money you made
From the drugs you sold that killed my child
Oh!, you say you are not responsible for what is done
    after the sale
All you do is supply, and after that,
You are gone, gone to spend the money
To buy big drinks, big cadillacs and fondle pretty women
You purchased a home, maybe in Beachwood
To get out of the ghetto, to get away from those who use
    the stuff
And those who turn on innocent children
You don't want your family exposed to such violence
You don't mean no harm—you say, just making a living—
    you say

Well Mr. Dope Man, let me plant a bug in your ear
You hit her, you killed her, and you are still killing
Aren't you ashamed, doesn't it bother you at all that you are
Turning out those babies
You say it doesn't bother you none, all you want is the fast
    cash
Big Cadillacs, pretty women and big drinks
To sip by the side of your big pool as you lay in the heat
    of the sun

Well, I want something too
I don't want the fast cash
I don't want the big Cadillacs
I'm not interested in the big drinks
And pretty women don't excite me none

What I want is you off the streets, you out of our lives
You out of the lives of the innocent ones
The ones you are destroying, the ones you are
Killing, the ones you make kill

Yes, Mr. Dope Man you killed my child,
Cause you sold the man the dope, that made him lose
    it all
And brought him to the point where he thirsts for young
    blood . . .
Innocent blood
Am I right or wrong, Mr. Dope Man?

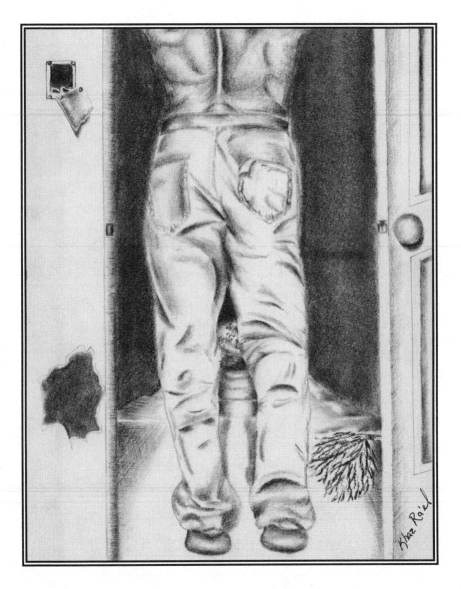

Ain't It A Shame

Ain't it a shame, child
How that man hit that poor little Gloria across her head
   like that
They tell me that he even raped her down them stairs
Lord have mercy on that poor innocent child

They tell me she was on her way to school, wasn't bothering nobody
I hear that she was even getting a perfect attendance
   award that day
Ain't It A Shame

I'd like to catch the critter that did it,
He ought to be strung up
No child, that's too good for him,
They ought to let them uncles get him
OOH!! Girl, I can see it now, if they do, won't be nothing
   left of him

Wonder why he had to bother that poor innocent little
   girl
Wonder why he had to bother anybody
Didn't have nothing better to do, maybe
It's that dope that these people are using
Yes, that's the reason they are acting so crazy
Whatever the reason,
He shouldn't have hit her like that

Tell me she was a good child, a cheerleader
A member of all kinds of sports
Yeah, if he had only left her alone,
She could have gone to the Olympics, you reckon,
No tellin, I heard that she sung in her church choir
Her mom declared that she was her right arm
She would keep the house clean, take care of the youngsters
And even respected her elders
Hush girl, don't tell me no more, you're bringing tears to
    my eyes
Don't make kids like that now-a-days, nope,
Not like little Gloria

What a terrible waste, she was so pretty too
I tell you something, every day it is something else
Don't even want to watch the news no more, too much
    tragedy
Poor little Gloria, poor little Gloria
Where you going child, why you going in the house
To pray, that's what I'm going in to do, to pray child
Pray for the mamma of poor little Gloria
That whoever did that to that child will surely give himself up

Ain't it a shame the way he eats and sleeps as if he didn't do it.
Ain't It A Shame!

Part II

The Anguish

Behind the Death of a Child

There are so many unfamiliar feelings
I see her everywhere but yet she is nowhere
I look for her always, I am even tempted to call out her name
Wish this boulder would get off my chest
Wish this tension would leave me alone
Wish this pain and loneliness would rest somewhere else
Or do I
No, not really, don't want this feeling to be on nobody

OOP! A glimmer of a smile slipped through my shut
    tight lips
Ain't supposed to smile *Behind the Death of a Child*
Wonder what the kids are thinking, wonder what they are
    feeling
I know that they are feeling something, but don't know what
Who knows anyway, they don't, neither do I

Wonder if they blame me, mamma it's all your fault,
She ain't here no more
Wonder do I blame me, wonder do I blame you,
Wonder do I blame God
Wonder if there is anyone around to put the blame on

Such unfamiliar feelings *Behind the Death of a Child*
Not a word has been invented yet to describe the feelings
Pain let go of my heart, loosen your death grip on my heart
Won't you go away, won't you ever go away
Pain such a heavy hand you have

I don't know, maybe you can describe it better than I
These feelings that come *Behind the Death of a Child*
Maybe I'm not doing such a good job of it,
If you can describe it,
If you can explain it,
Then this line is yours _____!

Insanity's Eyes

I looked into the eyes of insanity
And I'd like to tell you just what I did see
When I looked into the eyes of insanity
Insanity's eyes looked beautiful to me

For safe within the eyes of insanity
Appeared a place of refuge, a place to hide
At that time his eyes seemed to offer comfort
As he out stretched his arms open wide

Yes, for a brief moment, he showed me the easy way out
After all, life seemed so cruel and unfair; this was no
    doubt
His eyes seemed never ending, no figure nor form
As I looked even closer, his eyes seemed quite warm

I saw plenty of space to move around in,
A place to finally be free
They offered a place of consolation
Safe within the walls of insanity

So as I looked into the eyes of insanity
And pondered over just what my next move should be
I glanced momentarily in another direction
And noticed my children looking at me

I felt the pull from within their eyes
As if to scream at me, Mommy please don't go
For if you leave with insanity
Who will care for us, we'd need to know

As I stood there for a few brief moments
Being pulled, tugged and torn apart
I glanced then upward toward heaven
And let this prayer spring forth from my heart

Oh God, I prayed, please help me
For I am certain that you are aware
How I long to go with insanity
Please illustrate to me, that you still care

As the tears met beneath my water soaked chin
Suddenly, the strength came to me
To turn in the direction of my children
And wave good-bye to insanity

The tears blurred my vision as I glanced again at insanity
And you will never guess this time, what I did see
That shielded behind the warm eyes of insanity
Was a ferocious beast waiting to destroy me

So I dried my tears, which had now rapidly begun
And stepped into the direction of my daughter and my son
As I reached my destination, I rejoiced in the victory
For then I realized that insanity had not gotten me

As I relate this story to you,
At one time you might have even seen his eyes
Just don't trust a word he says,
For insanity tells loads of lies

For his promises that he offers, he is not able to keep
And he can only get to you if into his eyes you look deep
So as he tries to persuade you to come and go his way
Remember my little incident, and waive good-bye to
     insanity on that day

I FOUND NO CONSOLATION
IN INSANITY'S EYES!

These Feelings Are Mine

My feelings are mine
Why should I share them with you
Why should I attempt to express that which is locked in
   my soul
You ask, but do you really want to know
The truth is I don't know,
Never felt these feelings before
Gray is my color now, gray trees, gray grass, gray skies
Seems fitting just to see everything as gray

I want these feelings out, I'm trying to get them out
But they won't budge, they are always there
Pulling, pushing, tugging and tearing at my heart
This is my cross to bear, you want to help me
You say how can you do that, are you God,
Can you bring her back, no you can't,
Can you turn back the hands of time, no you can't
Can you make it December 5th the day before, no you can't
So why should I share my feelings, you can't do anything
   about them.

Go ahead, tell me about time again
How it will all be better in time
What about now, I will never forget,
The feelings will never go away
They are here to stay
How can I share them with you
Don't you understand that
These Feelings Are Mine!

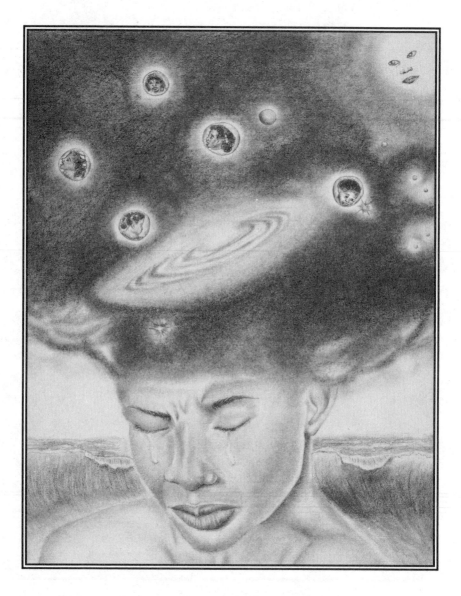

What Manner of Pain Is This?

What manner of pain is this that does not seem to cease
Such a strange and peculiar pain
Painful memories wrapped in painful experiences
Time does not seem to heal this pain
What Manner of Pain Is This?

I've grown use to covering the pain
So you don't see it, that is
Which only makes it worse
I really want to tell you about it
What Manner of Pain Is This?

Do you know where Gloria is
Can you tell her that I am looking for her
Can you tell her how badly I want to see her
Can you tell her how badly I want to put my arms
    around her
To hear her voice, even if it's only to say to her
Please be quiet Gloria

Can you tell her of the emptiness in our lives since that day
How our lives will never be the same without her
Constantly in the refrigerator, tying up the phone lines,
And being underfoot
Can you please tell her of this pain
"What Manner of Pain Is This?"
You don't know either, do you?
It's my cross to bear!

Don't Want To Laugh

Ha Ha Ha, you may hear me bellow out
It's not really a laugh
I make it up, cause I don't want to laugh

I don't feel right laughing
What is there to laugh about any way
Don't really find nothing funny

Oh, I can put up a good front
And a good back too
Because these feelings are mine
I have met fear
Now ain't that a shame

Maybe if you leave me alone I will laugh
Maybe if you don't worry so much about me, you will
    laugh
But right now, I don't want to laugh
For everything there is a season
A time to laugh, and a time to mourn

It is not my time to laugh
Won't you please let me mourn
I want to wallow in it,
I want to lay down in it
I want to blame myself
Cause maybe if I would have only . . .
Only what, only what . . .
What could I have only done

Well, I will laugh one day when all the hurt is gone
When I stop blaming myself, when I stop blaming you
When my color is no longer gray, and green comes to
    vision again
But right now all you see is a very good front
Because I don't want to laugh.

The Night

Too silent for me
No movement, only the thoughts moving around in my
    mind
No one to talk to only the thoughts moving around in my
    mind
No place to go, no place to hide,
Only the thoughts moving around in my mind

Phone silent,
TV talking, while I sleep
What goes on, on the other side of the door
During the night

Much happier during the day,
Able to keep ahead of the night
No thought of graves filled with innocent children—
    only during the night
No thoughts of murderers on the loose—only during
    the night
Thank God, for Jesus, if it wasn't for Him
My nights would be one big nightmare!

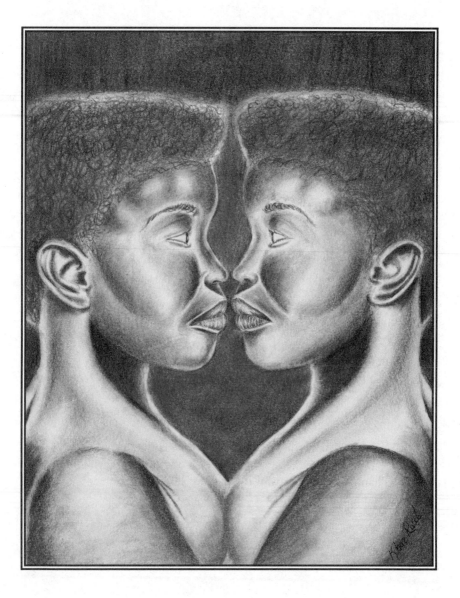

I Know Fear

I know fear
I've met him face to face
I've felt the cold touch of his icy fingers
I've heard the quivers in his loud, boisterous voice
He has no color, no form, not even a face
He has no morals, no scruples
He'll come in unannounced
He'll stay where he is not welcome, if you let him
He uses, abuses, and destroys those who let him stay
Boy! is fear ugly, he's mean, and really wants to scare me
    to death
He came to take me to my grave, that's it
Even though I've met him, I've seen his faceless form
I've felt his hand touch in my shattered life
He is not real
He's only a figment of my imagination
Without an ounce of real power!

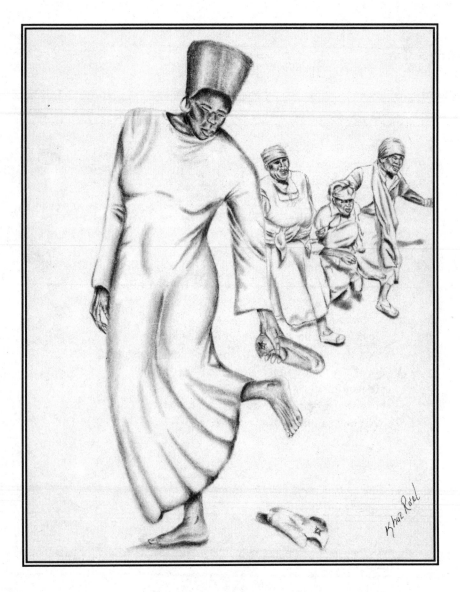

Take A Walk In My Shoes

Walk in my shoes for just a little while
And you will see that it is not as easy as you think
You will notice how tightly they fit
You will not be so quick to pass judgment against me

Walk in my shoes and you will see some of the directions
    that I go
Places that you would never go
Towards people whom you would never want to be
    seen with
the low, the depressed, the downhearted

Walk in my shoes for just a little while
Your whole opinion of me would change
You would bend forward, backward, and every way you
    could
To ask me kindly what can you do for me today or any day

You would notice first of all how worn these shoes are
How tired the feet inside of them are
That corns and bunions have rippled the sides of these shoes
You'd feel the weight of the state inside of them, seemingly
And yes, even the weight of the world

Just walk in these shoes, oh how different the
World would be to you
You would forget petty differences and gripes
Small would be big, and big would be small
Everything would matter, everything would mean
The world to you

The smallest gestures, the biggest thank you
The simplest note, that gigantic smile to the one
Who just passed you by

Mostly what you would see if you walked in my shoes
Is that there are two pair of feet inside of them
One pair belonging to me
And the other belonging to the one who walks right
    beside me

As a matter of fact, if you did walk in my shoes
You would be surprised to find out that they are
Not my shoes at all

Just loaned to me for a season
So I will pass them on to you when I'm done

Part III
The Mother—
"She's a Very Special Lady"

"She's A Very Special Lady"

The title of this chapter, "She's A Very Special Lady," is a perfect description of its author, a woman of courage, conviction and loving compassion.

It was a cold winter-like autumn day back in 1984 when I first came into contact with Yvonne Pointer. I was among the horde of both print and broadcast reporters, who along with family and friends, crowded into a small inner city church for the sad funeral of Yvonne's daughter Gloria Pointer.

Gloria had been brutally slain days earlier and I had seen Yvonne on various news broadcasts. During those broadcasts I began to see her inner strength and courage. At a time when the intrusion of the lights, cameras, and the callousness of hard-core newsmen can be trying, Yvonne handled the media with poise, answering every question no matter how difficult, and never wavering from her contention that her daughter's killer must be found.

But it was on the gray day of her daughter's funeral, amid the grieving and the heartache that always accompanies a loved one's final farewell, that I came face to face with this truly special woman.

The funeral was a particularly emotional one, the tears flowed freely. Even newsmen, hardened by daily exposure to the ills of our troubled society, had dampened eyes, and question on their lips wondering why . . . Why a child so young, so promising and so innocent had to die, or any child, or anyone.

It was during my coverage of the funeral, specifically the moment the coffin was removed from the church, that I suddenly worried about the well-being of the surviving mother.

As she was assisted down the church steps, her face grew as pale as the winter sky. Then doubled over in outward agony. Her strength, so evident prior to this moment, appeared sapped . . . the hurt and heartache. The emptiness of losing her oldest child had finally taken its toll. Desperate cries of "my baby," "my baby" . . . filled the air.

At that moment Yvonne Pointer had lost control. This image of a grieving mother, torn apart by the senseless murder of her precious child, was repeated that night on the evening news. It was an unforgettable scene. One that graphically illustrated the indescribable pain of losing a child.

Almost a year had gone by when I next saw Yvonne. Once again she was the subject of a new story, but his one was far different. This time it was a positive story, one that even today is still not complete.

Yvonne Pointer had been selected to receive one of TV-8's "Jefferson Awards," an award given to Greater Clevelanders for their tremendous contributions to the community.

Yvonne received the award for her tireless work following her daughter's tragic death. A lot of people talk about doing it, but Yvonne had found a way to turn a negative into a positive. She had converted her grief into concern and compassion for others, working with organizations, other parents of murdered children, to form a support network to help make life easier for those families.

This woman, who until now was a struggling single parent, with little interest outside her home, had miraculously pulled herself up from the depths of unhappiness and self-pity, to emerge into the spotlight. A role model of courage, and an example for the world to see.

Her strength was evident, whether appearing on television, or speaking before groups, her message was crystal clear. It was indeed a warning, protect your children, don't let what happened to me, happen to you.

Sadly, even more children have been slain since that snowy day the body of Gloria Pointer was found several years ago, but her death has meant new life, indeed a rebirth of Gloria's spirit in the soul of her mother. Yvonne Pointer is determined, in fact she's convinced its her mission on earth to ease the pain of others. More than once she has contacted this reporter to acquire the names, phone numbers and addresses, some way to get in touch, to offer compassion to yet another family who had tragically suffered the loss of a child.

She knows the pain, she has lived the sleepless nights, she has felt the agony, and perhaps her deeds are a form of self-therapy, but they're effective, not only for Yvonne Pointer, but more importantly for those who like herself have experienced the ultimate tragedy of losing a child.

As a reporter you meet a lot of people, so many in fact that often names and faces sometimes escape you. But every now and then you meet someone who leaves a lasting imprint. A lasting impression, someone you respect, admire and look up to. Yvonne Pointer is that type of individual, she is without a question *"A Very Special Lady."*

Wayne Dawson

Ms. Yvonne Pointer said she felt honored that I accepted to do a few notes on her book, directed at those who have lost a love-filled child, and to prevent this from happening to children to come, to bring the awareness of the world in which we live of what is going on, and how to bring it to a stop. This is a problem that I consider the greatest tragedy in the country. Children are our future, without them, there is no tomorrow. How anyone can bring intentional harm to an unprotected young, is beyond me. Animals are not as cruel to their young, as we are to ours, and the sad thing is that it continues on. This is heartbreaking. Yet after losing her own daughter, Yvonne Pointer has done everything she possibly could, to bring a peace within, and alert everyone to the pain, and the misery one could suffer through their own loss of one of theirs. I have seen her stand proud with courage, with the faith of God beside her for our tomorrows, our children and not tremble, or stumble in her cause. No, Ms. Yvonne Pointer the *HONOR* is mine.

Lyn Tolliver, Jr.
WZAK Radio

I have recently become a grandfather, and as I play with and comfort my granddaughter, I am reminded of our responsibility to serve as protector, teacher and spiritual leader of those little ones who look to adults for the pursuit of happiness and a decent quality of life.

We must, as a society, accept responsibility and accountability.

You must continue your efforts, and constantly remind us all that we must demand more for our children.

I miss Gloria.

John Hairston

The Biggest Little Lady

Yvonne Pointer is a single parent and the mother of eight-year-old Denyelle, and sixteen-year-old Raymond Pointer. Yvonne is a homeowner and resides in Greater Cleveland. She is a full-time employee, college student, faithful church goer and a community activist. This description—I'm sure—fits someone you know also; however, Yvonne is an extraordinary lady.

I remember the first time I saw Yvonne which was over 20 years ago. She was coming down the aisle of the church laden with a broken heart and a contrite spirit. Jesus met her at the alter and blessed her soul. Blessed she has been ever since!

Even though Yvonne is blessed her life has had it's share of sorrows and persecutions. I have witnessed this courageous, God-fearing lady come through many of them.

The greatest experience of sorrow came to Yvonne on December 6, 1984, when her 14 year old daughter Gloria Pointer was raped and killed on her way to school. While the average person would have withered away by such a tragedy, Yvonne became and continues today to be a living example that God's grace is sufficient to take us through life's grave adversities.

Prior to this awful tragedy, Yvonne always made time for the least one to the greatest. And, since this awful tragedy . . . this already remarkable lady had founded a support group "Parents Against Child Killing," and spearheaded the organizing of the Gloria Pointer Annual Scholarship Award in the Cleveland Public Schools, of which her late daughter Gloria was a student. Yvonne is also founder and president of "Positive Plus" an organization whose main objective is to promote individuals toward the positive pursuit of their goals. Yes, Yvonne's life is full of challenges and obstacles—all of which she faces with a strength and courage that only God can give

In addition to her latest involvements of the support groups, public speaking engagements and even the writing of this book, Yvonne yet finds time to make a pot of old-fashioned soup for a sick neighbor, take it to them and feed them, council the troubled teenager and encourage the broken hearted.

In fact, as writer John Wesley so appropriately states it in the passage below, sums up my thoughts as to why I think Yvonne Pointer is the *BIGGEST LITTLE LADY* I know!

> *Do all the good you can,*
> *By all the means you can,*
> *In all the ways you can.*
> *In all the places you can*
> *At all the times you can*
> *To all the people you can*
> *As long as ever you can.*

Yvonne, may the Lord continue to energize you to go on as long as ever you can!

Love,
Gloria Comar

Another Days Journey

Another holiday season was approaching quickly. The evidence was all around. The bright Christmas decorations and the echoes of the holiday tunes resounding over the various radio stations. Who could ever forget Donny Hathaway's "This Christmas" or the Temptation's "Rudolph the Red Nose Reindeer." Yes, those were called the "good old days."

My thoughts are quickly shifting as the car slides to the left and then to the right abruptly. A quick reminder also of the season which is winter in Cleveland, the type of weather that transplants many Northerners to warmer climates. Brrrrrrr!, just the thought of slush, snow, cold bus corners and waiting on delayed buses sends chills through my petite frame. In order to survive the chill it is best not to dwell on it. Besides, I'd much rather focus on the soothing sounds of Christmas.

As my thoughts began to shift, I am once again made aware of how large the snowflakes are. I remember as a child, sticking out my tongue to catch a snowflake and then the joy of swallowing snow would swirl me around with ecstasy. Yes, what wonderful memories of snowflakes. Yet, bolted in another portion of my mind is a painful memory of huge snowflakes. For the morning of December 6, 1984, was so very similar to today.

I remember so vividly peering through the window of my home on the east side of Cleveland, Ohio at the snow covered ground. My thoughts were "Good grief! Where did all of that snow come from overnight?"

As I turned to Gloria, my oldest daughter, as any typical mother would, I told her "Get the boots, hat, scarf, gloves and all the winter gear. It looks like a blizzard has hit Cleveland." Equally typical was her teenage response, "Ah Mom, I don't want to mess up my beautiful hairstyle with a hat." Nevertheless, as the saying goes, the stronger one survived and she left home prepared for the winter elements.

How was I to know that as I watched her trudge through the knee high snow and round the corner, that this would be my last view of her living soul.

Gee, the streets are really slippery. I never realized that Channel 5 was so far away from my house. Is it really that far or is it the weather? I questioned myself. Or is it my distant thoughts that make this journey seem endless? Once again I have been asked to appear on the *Morning Exchange,* a local morning television program. I feel that they are a great group of people. My purpose for appearing is not to cast a shadow of grief over the city but to possibly instill a ray of hope in the despairing life of a family who has been so tragically victimized by a senseless murder of a beloved child.

I really hope that my hair holds up under this bad weather, I thought. Ummm, like mother like daughter (smile). I cannot recall the exact number of journeys such as this that I have traveled over the past years. The various television appearances, the community meetings, the public speaking engagements, the Cleveland Public School appearances to teach the children safety techniques and the church services all in the name of a safer world for our children.

Even now as I endure the severe weather, I once again push to the rear of my mind all the grief and hurts that accompanied the brutal murder of my child. Instead I bring forward this one and only thought . . .

> *"If it is to be,*
> *It's up to me*
> *A safer world*
> *For our children to be!"*

Yvonne Pointer

Sun Rays Massaging My Shoulders

How I enjoy you, the warmth that you rub on me
As I walk beneath you
Some complain of your heat
You just feel so good to me

Seems as if you caress my troubles away
I am glad to have you shine upon me
To walk beneath you
My hat is off to you, for you work a wonder in me
Sun Rays penetrating even my soul
I am glad to have you, I appreciate your massage

I realize that I will not always have you
I know that others have gone on
Who can no longer feel the warmth of your rays
The only thing that bothers me sometimes though
Is that you shine on the killer too!

I Believe

I believe in God
I believe that He is in control of all things
I don't question His mighty act
Although I will admit that I would like to

I will admit that I don't understand them
I will admit that I miss Gloria
But yet, *I Believe*

I believe that in his appointed time,
He will reveal, watch and see
It will happen according to my belief
That is why *I Believe*

Oh, you think that I am wasting my time by believing
Think I should just give up
Say that the killer is long gone
You will see, you will see,
That *I Believe!*

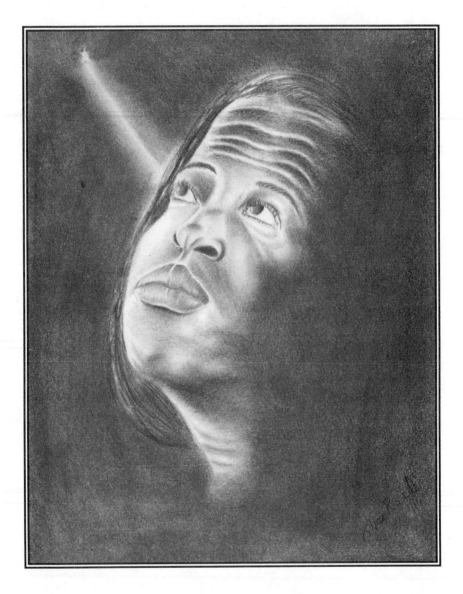

You Are My Reason For Living

You are my reason for living
You are with me whenever I call
You walk by my side, Oh how closely
You pick me up whenever I fall

Yes, you are my reason for living
When all of my hope has gone
I reached for someone to cling to
And each time I reached, I touched you

You promised that you would never leave me
You said that you would be my friend
I trusted you when trust was far from me
With you in my life I can win

You are my reason for living
I lift my tear stained eyes unto thee
And thank you for being my reason
and the mercy that you have shown me

What would I do without you
I don't dare even to try
For you are my reason for living
The one that wipes the tears from my eyes

Oh how badly my heart aches
And how much you know of the pain
Jesus it's you that has brought me
Your dying has not been in vain

Have you ever been lonely
Or have you just needed a friend
Well I know someone who will be there
Someone who'll guide from within

So turn your life over to Jesus
He's waiting just to answer your call
And He'll be your reason for living
He'll be there if you should fall

Yes, He is my reason for living
He's with me whenever I call
He walks by my side oh so closely
He picks me up whenever I fall

Conclusion

How appropriate it is to end this book with the writing of "You Are My Reason For Living" for truly in the course of losing a child there are long soul searching moments for a reason to even want to continue to exist (many of you understand perfectly well, what I mean). The days of deep discouragements, deep depressions, and endless sleepless nights seem to go on and on. But how glad I am to be able to say in the conclusion of this book, *Behind the Death of a Child,* that I do have a reason for living, and that time does help to ease the pain. I am deeply grateful in my heart to be able to share my most sacred inner thoughts with you because of the murder of my daughter, Gloria Pointer.

A very special thanks to Detective Janice Abernathy, who not only has been *A Bridge Over Troubled Waters* in my life, but has become as a member of my family. She has won a special place in my heart. When it appeared as if I had to walk alone in the investigation, she was there always praying and hoping—not to mention looking as well. God continues to be with her, as she continues to offer to other families the hope that she has given to me. Wayne Dawson, FOX Eight News, Lyn Tolliver, WZAK Radio, John Hairston, Gloria Comar, Khaz Ra'el for his contributing artwork, Denyelle and Spanky for being so special and you, the readers, for hearing my voice.

I hope that between the covers of this book you will find a line of hope that will enable you to survive.

Yvonne Pointer

The Gloria Pointer Scholarship was established in 1991. Annually, five hundred dollars is donated to an inner-city youth in the memory of Gloria Pointer towards his/her college education.

Proceeds from *Behind the Death of a Child* will enhance the scholarship funds.

The publication of *Behind the Death of a Child* was made possible through the generous donations and contributions of the following individuals:

Mr. David H. Beck, Something Special by David

E.F. Boyd & Son Funeral Home

Ms. Bridget Chapman

Dr. Robert Haynie

Mr. Ruben Holloway

Ms. Henia Johnson

Lakeside Place Limited Partnership

Mr. Jack and Ms. Gail Larson

St. Luke's Medical Center

Susan L. Taylor, *Essence Magazine*

Mr. Gil Walker